People Driven
SELLING

How to Sell More, Work Less and Have More Fun

CJ COOLIDGE, CBPA

People Driven Selling is a work of non-fiction. It consists of observations and impressions of the author gained during nearly 4 decades of selling a multitude of products and services. The lessons learned were the result of a most successful career as a Business Performance Advisor with Insperity. (NYSE:NSP)

Published in the United States by Longs Peak Press for
C4 Dynamics and CJ Coolidge, LLC.

Library of Congress Cataloging-in-Publication Data
Coolidge, Charles J.
People-Driven Selling: How to Sell More, Work Less
and Have More Fun / by CJ Coolidge

ISBN-10: 0981875831
ISBN-13: 978-0-9818758-3-5

Printed in the United States
www.cjcoolidge.com

First Edition

Motivate And Inspire Others!

"Share This Book"

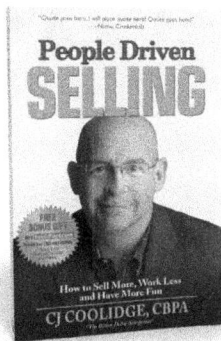

Retail $19.97

Special Quantity Discounts

5-20 Books	$18.97
21-99 Books	$16.97
100-499 Books	$14.97
500-999 Books	$12.97
1,000+ Books	$10.97

The Ideal Professional Speaker For Your Next Event!

Any organization that is committed to develop their people to become exceptional needs to hire CJ for a keynote and/or workshop training!

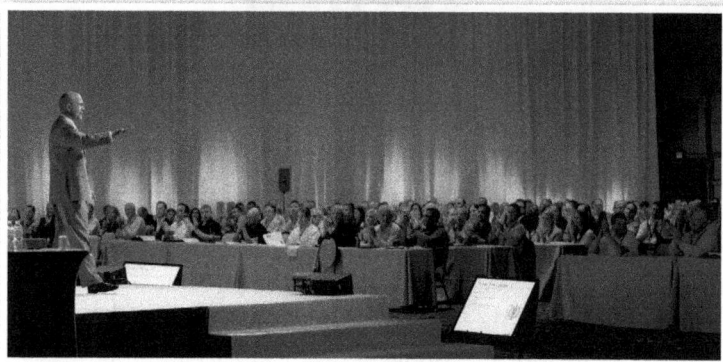

In Memory of my Father
Charles Joseph Coolidge Sr.
1926-2012

Dad was a salesman for over 60 years.
He never changed his approach, and it cost him a fortune.

His example and frustration encouraged
me to be flexible and resilient.
Dad, I can't thank you enough.
CJ+
2016

Contents

People Driven Selling:
Sell More - Work Less - Have
More Fun

Introduction

Life is about Connecting

"Instead of making your life about sales, make your sales about life."

Salesman. Just the word is enough to make some people shiver—even the salespeople themselves. Even if your career is specifically about selling a product or service, it is unlikely that you relish the idea of someone calling you a "salesman". This title has many negative connotations, especially in light of the manipulative and unsettling tactics commonly used in the contemporary market.

It does not have to be this way, however. You do not need to fall into the trap of fulfilling all of the clichés of the sales industry. Instead, focus yourself on becoming the type of person that naturally encourages people to recognize and take advantage of value and quality—rather than a person who is in it for himself. This concept has its roots long before you ever make your pitch. Instead of making your life about sales, make your sales about life.

To Live a Life Without Regret: Connect Early and Often

A few years ago I remember getting a call from my 85 year-old dad from the hospital. He had a brain tumor, the nastiest of all brain tumors, something called a glioblastoma. These tumors act as their name suggests; they explode all over the brain. They can't much be dealt with. They have no curative therapy. They are 100% fatal. We also learned that dad also had prostate and lung cancer. It was not good news, but dad had to accept that he was dying.

Almost immediately Dad wasn't able to take care of himself, so he moved into my house. This man, who I hadn't spent a whole lot of time with since I was about 14 years old, who kicked me out of his house at 18, was now living in my house.

Soon I noticed something very unusual. First, this is a very emotional thing for him, and for me. He would say things like, "I'm glad to get to know you as an adult." That's strange. I would say things like, "Pop, I'm middle aged. I'm 55. I could retire." This idea surprised him.

It's emotional because he's reconnecting. For 30 years, he hadn't had much to do with my family or me. He never got to know my spouse, so for him, it's really unusual. For me, his presence is also unusual, emotionally.

But, I was noticing something else. He was a hard-driving entrepreneur who had sold his business about two years earlier. He had been out of business only that long, not working only that long. You know what seemed strange? He talked, but he didn't talk his business at all. What do you think he talked about?

He talked about life. When he talked about life, he talked about people. He talked about his relationships. He talked about his relationships with his mother and father, his wife, and his children. He talked about his relationships with his clients, and with the other people he did things with.

In other words, the truth of the matter – though we say it, we don't recognize it – is that nothing really matters in the end except for the relationships that we build. Obviously, family relationships are foremost. But the relationships we develop outside of family, relationships in and around our business with clients, vendors and employees are no less important. These relationships also matter in the end.

So, it follows that it would be of significant benefit to recognize that when you're out there doing business, making connections, and selling things, you acknowledge that you're not a "widget producer" offering contracts to some inhuman entity that has a checkbook. You are a business, a company, an enterprise consisting of individual humans, a collection of people, volunteering in common mission to create, develop, produce, and deliver products and services that make life better and easier for other people. At the core, that's what business is.

You've probably experienced sales people coming to you trying to sell you something without knowing anything about you. They didn't have a clue whether there's any benefit for you. They're just "doing their job." They just want a deal. They just want to make their numbers.

Sometimes it feels as though they're just trying to ram something down your throat, like it's all about them, their needs, and their numbers. It's as if they're not even considering a relationship.

It doesn't have to be this way. In fact, things could work a whole lot better if it wasn't. When it comes to a high value life, strong, healthy contributing relationships are everything. The same is true for life in business.

Strong relationships make business and life a joy. You would sell more, work less, and have more fun.

CHAPTER 1

Getting Connected

Recruiting Good Sales People and Profitable Prospects

"By encouraging people to work in their areas of strength, avoiding their areas of weaknesses employees can create great results without burnout."

Your success is dependent on your ability to attract sales people who will actually care about your business, your goals your outcomes, your objectives and your numbers as much as you do.

These are the sales people who, because they care and connect, will produce month in and month out regardless of the state of the economy. These are the sales people who will actually care that the clients they develop are actually profitable. These are the sales people who care about the margins. They care about your enterprise.

These are the only kind of salespeople you want.

What kind of clients do you want? How can you find them?

How can you find prospects who want to have a meeting with you, and not just any meeting, but a value creating meeting? How will you find people who care to engage with you in a way that you will be able to effectively make a difference in their world?

These are the kinds of things that you have to start understanding in order to improve in your world of selling. When you find and connect the right kinds of people, they will naturally choose to buy from you.

These are things I discovered and will share with you in this book.

From Failure to Success: My Story

There's something distasteful about selling. I know. I have lived in the selling world for over 35 years now. During those years I have seen all kinds of manipulation, selfish deal making, and other abuses to risk tarnishing the profession forever.

For this reason even the idea of selling made me uncomfortable. Part of the reason for my discomfort is that I'm dysfunctional. I'm even "disabled" as a salesperson. I have all kinds of deficiencies. I'm scared of a lot of things. I don't handle rejection very well at all. I fail when I try to make cold calls. I'm very uncomfortable with the phone. I hate to interrupt a person's day. I'm disorganized. I lose things. I lose paper. I forget to follow up. I show up in people's offices and I don't have all my stuff. I have Attention Deficit Disorder and have a hard time staying on track. Truth be known, I'm deficient in most of the qualities we believe are essential for successful salespeople.

My dysfunction and disability used to present a real problem for me.

About 25 years ago, I partnered with a friend of mine to form a company to offer sales training. We figured that I would be good at this because I was a pretty good sales theorist. Besides, I had been selling somewhat successfully in my previous career.

Not so this time. Things didn't work out for either of us. In fact, it only took him 90 days to label me a complete sales failure. Prospects would say things like, "Send anybody - just don't send CJ." No kidding. He had to do something. So, without notice, he fired me. I finished a program. He walked in, said we were through. He did not offer to pay the last check that I felt he owed me. He would not cover any of my accrued expenses.

Suddenly I'm in trouble. I'm unemployed. I'm broke. I have three little kids and a spouse at home depending on me. I'm scared to death, and I've just failed at the only thing I think I'm remotely qualified to do.

There I was, cold, scared, and alone. I was at a crossroads. As I said, selling was all I thought I was qualified to do. I knew my weaknesses. I knew my fears. The time was short. I had to figure my way out. I needed an answer. I needed to find a way to sell successfully that didn't require me to become "Super Sales Guy," or to fix my weaknesses, and I needed to find it fast.

By grace, I did.

It was 1989, and I had the good fortune of meeting Paul Sarvadi, the founder of Administaff, now Insperity, (NYSE:NSP) Back then the company was in its infancy. Paul presented the farfetched notion that Insperity would change the way America does business, by helping business leaders better align and engage their workforce, with the result that their companies would run better, grow faster and they would make a lot more money.

I was thunderstruck. Paul was sharing his company's world-changing vision, and recruiting at the same time. No one had ever talked with me about things like this before. I'd always heard that I was supposed to trade my time for money. I was supposed to "get a job" and to sell things "*to*" prospects. No one had ever suggested that that a company existed to contribute, to make a difference. No one ever had presented the idea that I could or should do the same.

Well, a spark was lit that day. I wanted to change the world, too. I wanted to matter. I wanted my work to matter.

It didn't matter to me that our prospects knew nothing about what we did. I didn't care. I would be on a mission to change the world.

Paul offered the position with Insperity, but not until they had put me through a regimen of pre-employment tests. These tests proved providential in that they exposed my weaknesses and revealed my strengths. The test showed (like it was news to me) that I couldn't manage my way out of a paper bag. Ouch. However, on the positive side, the same test showed that I could inspire. Cool.

Insperity management offered an amazing deal. The position would be for business development with 100% commission.

I would inspire, and my managers would handle the administrative work for me. The rest is history. The results were unprecedented.

By encouraging people to work in their areas of strength, avoiding their areas of weaknesses employees can create great results without burnout. The company can make a fortune, too.

Over the course of the next few years as Insperity made the list of Fortune companies, I contributed literally a billion dollars in revenue. For at least eight of those years, my accounts were the company's most profitable. As a result, for several years Insperity actually named their annual profitability award "The CJ Coolidge" award. What is most amazing about this is that I accomplished all this working less than 25 hours a week, maybe nine months a year.

What I learned are the most exciting and breakthrough insights for selling to come around in years.

And in this book, I want to give them to you. I want to help you start selling comfortably and naturally while sending any "slick and slimy salesperson" imagery you may have away forever.

The Essentials: What You Need to Succeed

The book has four basic sections:

1. In the first section, I will show you how natural selling is really synonymous with life. Then I will show you three powerful but under rated and overlooked life principles that align so closely with selling, that, when applied, could improve results and satisfaction immediately and exponentially.

2. In the second section, I will briefly explore the three biggest myths held by salespeople, prospects and managers. Believing and adhering to these myths make salespeople lose approachability, credibility, and efficiency. These myths, when applied, actually prohibit prospects from making the most of every transaction.

3. In the third section, I will help you to redefine your idea of value. In this section I will explain "the one thing that all prospects desperately want and if you gave it to them, they would clamor to meet with you all day long."

4. In the fourth and final section, I will define "natural selling" and "the power of pull." Here we will explore how to get more meetings, how to make them more productive, and how to lead prospects to take action. This will give you great insight into things to really improve your efficiency and profitability.

If you are interested, I won't need to sell you anything. That's a good thing.

CHAPTER 2

Natural Selling is Life

"The body is not a battery. It doesn't have energy. The body is a power plant. A power plant does not "have" energy, it generates it."

—*Brendon Burchard*

Here's an interesting and daring observation. Natural selling and life are exactly the same things. Life is selling; selling is life.

That's not how we see it. You've heard people say things like, "I don't like to sell. I don't want to sell. I hate to sell. I'm not going to sell. That's for those (slimy) salespeople." There's a reason for that and I'll explain it to you in a minute.

Consider an idea about life and human interaction. Human beings are unique. Each human being experiences life differently from every other human being. Human beings have different perspectives of things all around them. And, in the course of human interaction, there is communication. What lies at the core of all human communication? The unique perspectives of each individual.

It could be said that any shared idea is an attempt to persuade. Why else would anyone ever share a position? Sharing an idea, a belief, a perspective is one human's attempt to connect with another and to influence the dialog. Anything worth sharing is worth at least a nominal attempt to persuade.

When any unique person's idea about things is shared with another person, there is an encounter. It is an encounter of ideas. And, since no two ideas or perspectives are ever exactly alike, the encounter produces friction. It is friction in the areas of difference between the unique perspectives. Another word for this friction is *argument.*

In a well-engaged society of even two people, communication consists of the sharing of unique perspectives. Often there will be a difference between the perspective of the hearer and the speaker. Both participants make effort to persuade toward their unique position. The goal is recognition of a common position. If the communication is open, honest and engaged, the effort to establish an agreeable common position will follow. This effort, quite simply, is argument.

From this perspective, arguing is the centerpiece of human interaction. It is good. It is necessary. It is healthy. It is essential. But we have created a stigma to argument. We've made it bad. We've made it distasteful.

The negative spin on argument comes because not

every effort to establish an agreeable common position can be successful. Sometimes the backgrounds, maturity, experience, perspective of the involved parties are so different that common ground is impossible to discover. In a perfect world both parties could simply agree to disagree, but human pride and selfishness gets in the way. This is why argument has become a dirty word.

We argue selfishly. We argue to get our point across and to push others to conform, acquiesce or agree. We argue as intellectual bullies. We argue to "win," to be proven right by proving another wrong, and in the process, we expect ego gratification at the expense of another person. What's worse is that many times we argue to beat our "adversary's ideas to a pulp," diminishing them thoroughly, thus establishing our position as unshakably superior.

There has to be a loser. Someone must go down.

We also don't always keep the argument on the level of ideas. Often even in a well-initiated verbal argument, sensing that our idea may be losing weight, we feel some ego damage approaching, and move to defend. But it is now our egos we are defending, not our ideas. Defensiveness takes the argument away from the field of ideas into an intentional attack on the other person, and their ego. We may not be able to defend our idea, but we sure won't feel like a loser either.

After some years of this, it's easy to understand why people would rather avoid argument or confrontation.

Relationships and connection are really as important as we suggested earlier. Belonging and acceptance are vital human needs. Since many arguments degenerate into the loss of both, it is easy to see how people start to behave in such a way as to avoid argument or potential disagreement, which could lead to an argument. No one wants to risk ego damage. No one wants to risk being diminished. No one wants to risk a loss of acceptance and belonging.

The problem here is that this behavior actually diminishes the value of individuals and the relationships rather than strengthening them. It creates people who can barely exist together.

The only way to never argue then is to never share a belief or a position about anything at least not an important or significant belief or position. Hence the proverb: Never discuss religion or politics.

Selling and Argument – Synonymous

It's no wonder people don't like selling.

Every sales encounter requires an exchange of ideas. Every idea worth sharing is worth challenging. Every challenge is an argument and we know now how most arguments end.

What is life with relationships if not the opportunity to interact? What is the purpose of interaction if not to share ideas and perspective? What good are we together if not iron sharpening iron? How worthless would life be if ideas couldn't be proposed and argued?

We need to get over the idea that argument is bad. It is actually essential. We need to begin to shift our approach to argument from winning to understanding. We need to learn to argue for our position by understanding each other, to become clear about one another's perspective so that we may communicate our position within that perspective. Then, in the collaboration of shared ideas, all our ideas can be enhanced and improved, relationships will be strengthened, and egos spared.

Each individual is important. We all know and believe different things. We should believe our ideas are important, too. From that perspective, how should we interact? We should share our ideas and we should expect that when we share them, we will come up against different positions. This is good. This is life. If we care about others, we won't have to *push* them into anything; we are merely expressing life, expressing beliefs and ideas. Such is argument at its core. Willingness to argue (unselfishly) is of tremendous value as it expresses the greatest respect and love for others. It tells another human being, "I value and believe something enough that I will share it with you, at personal risk."

Isn't this just another form of selling?

I think it is. It adds so much to life. It is natural.

Let's look at 3 fundamentals to life and to selling. Each of these must be intentionally and carefully nurtured because each of these tends to naturally diminish with age and experience.

Fundamental 1: Nurture Flexibility

James Canton, author of *The Top Trends That Will Reshape the World in the Next Decade,* said, "The greatest barrier to future success is past success." Now, that seems to be a contradiction. We actually tend to believe the opposite.

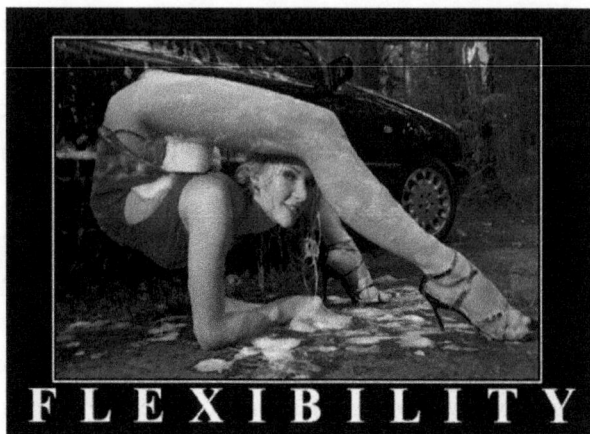

F L E X I B I L I T Y

We have this idea that just because something worked before, it should continue to work again. This behavior is the result of inflexibility. As it pertains to selling, we think that just because we sold a certain way in the past, the same method should work today. Flexibility is something that really must be nurtured. As each of us gets older, we lose flexibility. We start to think, "I'm not ready or creative enough to change something I've done this way for a long time. "

I've experienced three shifts in selling models since I started selling. We're about to enter a fourth one that is an entirely different one from anything we've ever approached. In this 4th shift, flexibility will be more important than it was for any of the previous models. It doesn't matter how old you are. Get flexible or you're going to struggle selling in your organization.

Here's just one HUGE part of the shift that has already occurred, but that few have noticed. It is the prospect's shift from a preference for written, printed information to a preference for video. It is the shift from a preference to read, to a preference to watch.

Consider Google and YouTube – which is the most active search protocol today?

It's YouTube. Even though YouTube searches exceeded Google's back in March of 2011, I know that 90% of businesses I work with are still communicating in letters, brochures, still pictures and written copy. The first reason is that most are not aware of the change. But that's not the worst. The biggest reason is inflexibility. We're not flexible enough to accept the change. We're too fearful to do a video. "We're not actors!" We aren't flexible enough to adapt. We aren't comfortable putting ourselves out there so someone can look us in the eye and have us tell them what it is that we do that's of the highest value to them. (It's too much like setting up an argument, right?)

But the future's not going to be as vital for companies who hide behind words on paper. Your customers and prospects will prefer video. They won't have time to read what you write, and you won't have time to read what your suppliers write, either. The old methods will waste your time and money because they won't connect.

My program participants will often validate the truth behind what I'm saying. They'll brag that their company spends a lot of money producing videos, and that the impact is worth the expense.

I tell them that they can get the same outcome at a fraction of the expense, not to mention time and effort, if they would just get comfortable doing simple direct to the camera video on their own.

The world is not looking for polished, perfect commercials because polished commercials don't usually connect. Today's savvy prospects don't believe polished, perfect commercials. Prospects are people. People want real. People want credible. People want you. People want video. Video will trump printed brochures and static web pages for conversion and interest every time, and for the rest of your life. That said, just about any video will work a lot better than any brochure you have up on the web.

By the way, within the next 18 months, Google will entirely shift their search algorithm from today's SEO models to a relevance model. If you continuing to use SEO, you'll be left behind. Google will be looking to rank materials that are current, well read and recommended. It's a train that has already left the station. Another sign of our natural and growing inflexibility is the amount of time it has taken most companies to get involved in email marketing. I am watching companies just now getting savvy in email's use as a marketing vehicle. That's kind of sad considering that email has already reached maturity as a medium. It is already being replaced. Many universities no longer give email addresses to their students. Why? Because the students are use social media and text messaging for critical correspondence.

Why does business always seem to stay a step behind?

Businesses are typically inflexible.

Fundamental 2: Nurture Resilience

Resilience, like flexibility, gets tougher with experience and maturity. But in these hyper-dynamic times, it is no less necessary. As we mature, and attempt more things, and take risks, we fall down and get beat up. Resilience is essential to survival.

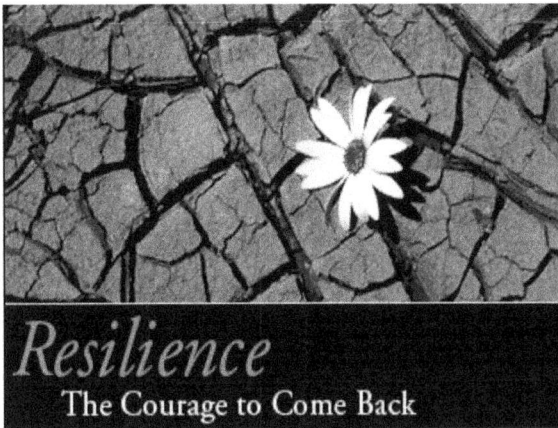

Resilience
The Courage to Come Back

You have to be resilient enough to stand up again any time you get knocked down. If you're going to be bold enough to share your ideas, you're going to get knocked down.

What's more, if you become flexible enough to try new things you will certainly need an abundant supply of resilience.

Resilience will be required any time you attempt to work with a business model or a business venture that's different than what you've done before. It's unavoidable that you will make mistakes. You may hire someone you shouldn't have. You may over promise and under deliver. You may attempt systems and processes that just don't work. You may even lose your shirt. Just like with flexibility, we start to lose touch with some "natural resilience" we may have had when we were younger. We start to experience that when we risk and fail, it becomes harder and harder to get back up.

No matter, the future is going to require resilience more now than at any time in the past. It doesn't even matter if you're right.

Bill Gates says, "A new idea has the shelf life of a banana." That means you should expect to be knocked down even in the things that you start to do correctly.

If you're going to nurture resilience, you must lose your belief that you know all you need to know. You will have to assume the role of a lifelong student. You may have once believed that your college career was all the education you'd ever need. Those days are gone. It is not. You will need to start reading more than you ever have, investing in training more than you ever have, and growing, too. The knowledge you're going to need tomorrow is knowledge you don't have today. It is new, and that's okay... unless you don't want to be resilient.

You're a smart person. You have the ability to go out and pursue new information, but not if you're bogged down in the details of running your company every day, and you've got a whole sales force of folks who don't have time to read anything because they're too busy making calls, or people who are so busy working that they don't invest time to develop themselves.

This lack of developmental focus will lead to demise in this world where the value you'll need to maintain profitability will come from the new things you learn and apply. Resilience makes this possible.

Fundamental 3: Nurture Stamina and Energy

If you want to be able to keep things working profitably, you will certainly need a lot of energy and stamina. It goes without saying.

However, just like Flexibility and Resilience, we tend to lose Energy and Stamina as we age. The good news, here is that it doesn't have to be that way. The expected decline in both stamina and energy is based on poor habits, and even poorer teaching. We've all been given bad information, and it is costing us our health and vitality. We've been taught the wrong things about energy – what energy is and how energy works.

Let me explain a little about physiology and energy. We have the idea that when we wake up in the morning and we're still a little tired, we need to get a cup of coffee, to kick start and stimulate the system. We expect to do something similar at two o'clock in the afternoon when we feel that little energy lag. We eat cookies, or drink some energy product. Or get more coffee. No kidding.

We believe that when we get home and we're tired that we need to go to sleep, get a rest, or have a drink.

We do these things because we believe that our body is a battery, that it has energy, and that we recharge it by sleeping or by adding something like caffeine. We have been taught that bodies "store" energy.

Here's a more accurate idea. Marketing Guru, Brendon Burchard says, (and proves during his 4-day marathon events) "The body is not a battery. It doesn't have energy. The body is a power plant. A power plant does not "*have*" energy, it generates it." Think about that. The body is not a battery that has energy. It is a power plant that generates energy.

How does the body generate energy? No one ever taught you this. They told you to jump start with coffee. They didn't teach you that you have the ability to create a lot of energy yourself. No one ever told you that your body is a power plant.

Creating energy requires only a few items. Like with fire, only a few items are required – like 3. Fire requires fuel, oxygen, and heat. The body requires the same, plus one more, to generate energy.

First, it requires fuel. Fuel – most of us have plenty of that.

(Just grab your waste line and see!) Not all fuel is as good as others, but for the sake of our discussion, fuel is readily available to most of us.

Next, is oxygen. Again, for the most part, oxygen is readily available. The last two things required for the body to generate energy are water (80% of our bodies are made of this) and heat. I'll explain how this works in a minute. If you have water, oxygen, fuel and heat, you can generate energy at most any time that you need it. Every one of us has the ability to become totally engaged, totally focused, totally present, fully energized in any moment we need during our workdays. We just don't know how to generate it ourselves.

Of course there are exceptions for things like ill health, or abuse, or after extreme exertion when periods of recovery are essential. But during an average day, energy is available at any time.

By the way, who deserves energy from you?

Replace with:

Imagine coming home after a long day at work. You're beat. You walk in the door and you see your spouse. Since you're tired, you sigh and slump in the chair without engaging. You see your child, or your teenager and you do the same. This is a travesty. My 85-year old father would wish for such an opportunity. He was living with me, and wishing that he had generated the energy to connect back when he should have. He wished that he had known this principle when he had the health to apply it. Now he had regrets. Had he known better, when he came home from work each day he would have stopped, realized the importance of connecting, and he would have energized himself because his family was worth his attention. Think about it. Your family is worth your attention. Now. Your spouse is worth your attention. Now. Your husband is worth your attention. Now. Your customer is worth your attention. Now. Your employee is worth your attention. Now. Not at some time in the future.

The idea that you have a meeting with one of your employees, and because you're a little tired or you're a little down, you aren't fully present, you're not fully engaged is a total waste, but we do it all the time. I know of bosses who sit appearing bored during scheduled meetings with their subordinates flipping through emails. This is pure disrespect, and way beneath their ability to deliver their attention, which is what is required in the moment. Anyone can marshal the energy. We just need to learn how.

You Can generate energy

As I said before, the elements required to generate energy in the body are fuel, oxygen, water and heat.

We have fuel. How are you with water?

Most of us are deficient here. Many of our headaches and other body aches are the result of living in a pre-dehydrated state most of the time. We don't drink enough water. Consider our habit of waking to a cup of coffee in the morning. After sleeping 8 hours (without replenishing your water supply) you wake dehydrated. Then, the first thing you do upon waking is to drink a diuretic, which takes water from you.

Stop. Dump the coffee and go for a liter or so of water when you first wake up. That's what your body needs.

Drinking a coffee diuretic is irrational, but we haven't been taught better. Next you need oxygen. You need to breathe better, fully, and often. You need to learn to breathe deeply, belly breath, as it is called. You need to start to breathe – to start to practice deep breathing.

Have you ever realize how shallowly you start to breathe throughout the day?

In fact, you should notice your physiology when you start to feel a little down, a little unmotivated, or tired. I bet your shoulders are a slumped and your breathing is shallow.

At that time, sit up – better, stand up. Inhale deeply. Hold your breath for a second and exhale slowly. Be controlled. Do this 5-6 more times. You'll feel better. It's unavoidable.

Finally, you need heat. This can be crated at most any time. Heat is generated by the movement of muscles. The larger the muscle, the greater the heat.

People ask me all the time where I get my energy while I'm speaking. That's easy. I've hydrated. I breathe deeply while I'm talking and I keep my large muscles engaged and moving. I can get myself excited by jumping up and down. I'm not just getting excited. I'm actually creating energy and you can do the same thing.

Here's an exercise you may use to generate energy.

Be sure that you are hydrated and breathing. Then, find your large muscles, like your core, your back or your quads. Then, engage them. Tense your back. Put you quads in motion with knee bends. Use these large muscles to produce heat.

Anytime before you go in to see a client or before you step into your house to see your loved ones, instead of dragging in, consider remaining outside, and focus on creating energy before you go in. Think, "I'm going to breathe, I'm going to focus, and I'm going to move large muscles. Then I'm going to go in and be fully present."

Most of your sales people probably don't know they can do this. If you believe that their sales success is tied to their making more calls, and you ignore the critical element of energy creation, you're missing the boat. You'll wear them out and rob them and your customer of the opportunity to produce the kind of value that leads to sales success. They need to have themselves energized. That is what's going to communicate and connect best with prospects.

I accomplished all those tremendous results for Insperity working what they thought was less than full-time because I was fully energized for EVERY call. I realized that I couldn't be fully energized ALL the time, so I planned for rest and recovery, too. (No one can maintain the highest levels of energy all the time.) There is an optimum amount of time where you can maintain these high levels after which recovery is necessary. This is a life cycle we often ignore which leads to burnout.

But you CAN be your best and most energetic just about anytime you choose to be. And once you know your optimum level and endurance, strive to maintain it every week. There is a diminishing return on all the investment beyond the optimal.

Our misunderstanding of these energy principles creates lower than necessary results, and unnecessary turnover. Our management practices don't allow our sales teams to become all that they could be. We encourage them work when they should be resting. They get burned out quickly.

Results aren't what they should be either, because overworked and un-refreshed sales people are not as energized or present as they need to be when with your prospects and clients.

They aren't really connected and alive.

—— CHAPTER 3 ——

Myths of Traditional Selling

Exposing What Selling is NOT

*"Perception is reality" is one of the most
dangerous and potentially deceptive of
any idea ever presented as beneficial to
any salesman."*

L et me expose some myths about selling. You know
these, by the way. They're myths because they are things
we believe, but aren't really true. These don't work. I'm
sorry – they do work. They can and do generate sales, but
they are just largely unnatural and are counterproductive
to the relationship.

Myth # 1 – Finesse
The first myth is the myth of finesse. It's the idea that you've
got to act and talk in a certain way, like a "trained salesman"

in order to be successful. This myth exposes our love affair with and dependence on sales technique. You read the books on how to sell. You learn the "Benjamin Franklin Close," among others.

One technique suggests that the most important word to any prospect is their own name. The technique suggests that the salesman should learn to repeat the prospects name throughout the sales interview. I don't know about you, but this technique used on me has always been an irritant. I always feel strange and on edge when someone uses my first name 20 times in a single paragraph. I feel like someone's trying to sell me something.

Have you ever sat across from a trained sales guy? I'm talking about a guy who is steeped in sales technique – slick, natural, quick. A guy who has seems to have a perfect comeback for everything, like the guy you deal with at the timeshare meeting. Have you ever sat there? How did you feel? He's so good in sales technique, but it's so artificial in the life connect technique.

This is a strange. No one likes to be at a closing with a closer. Yet the very thing we don't want done to us is the very thing we try to train ourselves and our sales people to do to somebody else. Does that make sense?

This is the most artificially connecting BS. It's stupid to go out and look like a sales guy. What do you think your prospect thinks? Are they prepared to push back just a little bit? Are today's prospects trained a little better in the anti-sales technique stuff? It's worth asking. This myth doesn't suggest that good psychology, preparation or training is not appropriate. On the contrary, these can be invaluable tools to assist in maximizing understanding and moving the argument along. What it does suggest is that any and all techniques must be subjugated to a genuine care for the benefit of the prospect and a desire to deliver real value.

Technique pales compared to being real, being honest, and being transparent. Just being people interested in helping make life better for other people. There's no smoke and mirrors here.

Myth # 2 – Fluff

The second sales myth is the myth of fluff. I believe that the

belief in this myth is the primary reason that the sales profession has such a bad name. I know that it was for me. The reason I was uncomfortable selling is that I felt I was expected to act like my training suggested, and I felt manipulative. I felt somewhat disingenuous.

Who wants to be that if you're going to be out in the world building relationships of value?

This myth is exposed in the sales concept I have always heard called, "Perception is reality." I'm certain you've heard the phrase.

"Perception is reality" is one of the most dangerous and potentially deceptive of any idea ever presented as beneficial to any salesman. Let me explain what I mean, as the concept itself is neutral, and accurate at its core. It simply acknowledges that what a person (prospect or anyone else for that matter) believes about a something is, for them, the truth, or reality. This makes sense.

It could have a positive side. The sales person, knowing this concept, would work doubly hard to make sure that what a prospect perceives is indeed the truth, not a skewed image of the truth useful to move the prospect to a close. It would be positive and relationship building if I make sure that what my client "perceives" is, in fact, what is "really real." Understand?

This is not how the concept is used in the typical sales world. Sales and marketing professionals have intentionally taken huge and disingenuous liberty with this concept. Rather than making sure that the prospects perceptions actually line up with truth, or reality, they manipulate those same perceptions attempting to create a false reality.

Used this way, and you know such is common, "perception is reality" means that the sales professional wants and even intends to develop any perception that may lead you to buy, even if the reality isn't exactly as you perceive.

- Does ShamWow suck cola out from under a carpet? No, it does not. (The false videos are exposed on YouTube.) ShamWow doesn't do that.

- Would your 401(k) not have tanked had you used E-Trade? Really?

- Does your Whopper look like the Whopper in the picture? Never.

- How many big fat dudes have that BowFlex thing in their garage, because 90 days from now they're going to look like Superman? It doesn't work like that.

- How many diets work? Think about it.

We have this idea that it is OK to not tell the truth. It happened as our economy developed, and most every product ant offering became almost universally saturated. Everyone already had most of what they thought they needed. The sales profession had to find an easy way to create the perception that they, in fact, did not. We didn't call creating false impressions lying; we called it puffing. Puffing has even been tested in the Supreme Court. Puffing: It's okay to exaggerate your claim "a little bit."

What did pandemic puffing do to the marketplace? It created a naturally existing disbelief in all prospects. Some call it "healthy disbelief." It's like acknowledging and accepting that no one is trustworthy. No sales person is trustworthy. Everybody lies.

What kind of a person wants that kind of reputation?

One of the problems with this situation is that it is very inefficient. It creates more work for all prospects in order to get to the truth about any offering. It's like saying, "I don't believe anything sales people tell me. I don't believe the claims in your advertisements and neither does anybody else." In fact, the research says that only 17% of your audience believes your advertising claims, anyway.

The real reason that everything you say about your company isn't believed by anybody is because we've lived in this world of "perception is reality" thinking, "I've got to cause you to buy something you don't even need," which is part of the problem with selling.

So how do a lot of prospects feel when being approached by a salesperson? "You don't care about me; why are you trying to ram some trash I don't need down my throat?" Since we all believe that's what everybody's doing anyway, we start cutting the people and their communication off.

Customers have a well-developed sense of distrust for every offer.

What happened to caring?

Myth # 3 – Force

The third myth is the myth of force. In this myth is the idea that selling is just a numbers game. The harder you work the numbers, the greater your success. If you don't have the results you want, you're not working hard enough.

At one time this notion was probably real. The market had not reached saturation in most offers, and there was no mass media. People were not on full time overwhelm. There was a time when people weren't all that busy, and the interruptions

could actually create a pleasant diversion. As it is today, everybody is already overworked and over-interrupted. That goes for your prospect, as well. Herbert Simon, who wrote about a thousand scientific papers and won a Nobel Prize in economics, accurately predicted the current situation forty years ago.

He wrote, *"What information consumes is rather obvious. It consumes the attention of its recipients. Hence, a wealth of information creates a poverty of attention."*

Do you know that your prospect has to guard his attention and can't just give it to you? If everybody in your workspace is already overworked, and all the prospects are overworked, and you need more sales and you believe that selling is a numbers game, what will you do? You'll just push your sales force out there to make more and more calls.

You're inflexible. You know this is the correct approach because it worked last time you needed more sales.

What if all your competitors do the very same thing at the very same time?

Try to imagine life, now, for your prospects? What does your prospect start to feel? What does he have to do?

He's got to guard himself against all of you. When you or another sales rep comes to interrupt a business owner, he has to protect his attention, and keep you out.

Think about yourself as someone else's prospect. Are you taking any defensive, precautionary maneuvers yourself? Are you deleting emails? Are you avoiding phone interruptions? Do you deny meetings?

How many e-mails do you think are getting through when you send e-mails out to market? A lot don't because your prospect does what you do: delete, delete, delete, delete, delete, delete, delete, delete... and delete, delete.

Here's what I think: "I don't have enough bandwidth for somebody to interrupt my day for something I don't need to hear about. Since I don't trust you anyway, and I think you're just trying to schlep me, I'm through with all of you." That's a common belief in the mind of an increasing number of prospects in virtually every market.

That's going to be more and more the case with your prospects. They have too much on their plate to listen to you the way you currently deliver using these little models here.

You CAN'T force your way into more sales.

CHAPTER 4

Truths of Natural Selling

Declaring the Truth

"Winning is making life better or easier for the people you work with. Every time. You can win the deal and still lose, and you can lose the deal and still win."

Do you know what clients and prospects really want? Can you deliver it to them in a way that makes their life or business better and easier? This is what selling really is. It's really that simple.

It comes down to this: You have to determine, then the prospect has to understand, how you, this meeting, your product, or your service will make life better for them in the present.

I've got to know. You have to know. There can be no doubt. We all have to know that this thing you're asking me to take part in is going to make life better for me.

This is interesting, because we don't think that way. Start asking:

- How does working with you make life better and easier for your prospects, customers, vendors or employees?

- How much do you or your salespeople care to do that? Your prospect is thinking about himself, his business, his customers, his employees, his vendors, and his numbers, all the time. Your prospect needs your help improving something he or she thinks about. Really.

It's a whole different world when I care that my vendor, my customer, my employee, or the person I'm talking to in effort to sell him something is actually going to be in a position where his life will be better because he met with me.

How many of you tell your sales people to get in there, lay their agenda out and get in and out in ten minutes like they're supposed to? "Your prospect doesn't have time to listen to you." Not true. If you're obviously investing in somebody's life and they're feeling it, they want you there longer. Do you know why? They need someone to invest in them. Nobody else is doing it. In fact, everyone else seems to be trying to take things from them.

If you want to stand out, start **connecting** with the people you talk to. Do it in such a way that they can feel love, and know that you're actually going to deliver something there. Then they can't resist you, because they need what you are offering desperately.

Natural Selling and The Power of Pull

This is an interesting concept: the power of pull. We talk about it a little, but most companies, however they talk about it, live by the power of push.

I'm going to characterize pull in a way that helps you know how you can get into a meeting, why somebody would want to listen to you, and why they'll ultimately want to buy from you.

Booker T. Washington said, "There are two ways of exerting one's strength: one is pushing down, the other is pulling up."

There are two ways to exert pressure. The first is the typical pressure we know in selling: pushing down. "I'm going to hammer you into a deal, and then I'm going to feel good about it." Isn't that how we see it? The second is not typical. "I'm going to listen and learn and see if I can recommend a way that working together, you will become a better, stronger, more profitable enterprise."

Booker T. Washington

When winning is "getting the deal," it is easy to see how pushing becomes our typical action. If you consider getting a deal a win, you're missing it. Getting a deal is not a win.

Winning is making sure that value is delivered in every encounter.

Winning is making life better or easier for the people you work with. Every time.

You can win the deal and still lose, and you can lose the deal and still win.

But the issue is "Did I make life better for this person?" If the answer is yes, that is a win 100% of the time. It is not a win if I get a deal. A deal is gravy because I won when I knew that I really made life better for my prospect.

So in the process of selling, I need to be out there primarily to make life better for someone else. That's what I want to care about.

Selling: Pulling People Up

Increasing your prospects ambition is a valuable and worthy goal.

When selling, do you ever think of yourself as trying to pull someone up to a higher level of their own performance, a higher level of their own aspirations, a higher level of their own view of themselves, of the world?

Do you have the ambition to understand and communicate how working with you will bring them to this place of their own higher self-awareness, self-achievement, or self-fulfillment?

That's way different than focusing on whether you get a contract or how much money is involved. It's a bigger, more fulfilling picture, too.

Natural Selling: Lift Prospects to New Heights

I want to show you how to have people want to meet with you, how to have them want to listen to you, and how to have them want to buy from you. How do you create clients?

I use the word *"client"* very specifically here. What does

client mean, and how is client different from customer? Customer is someone who buys from you – someone who participates in a transaction. What's a client? A client is somebody you have chosen to shepherd, or to protect. A client's business is one you are committed to cover and protect. A client is someone you commit to help.

Here is what you should be able to say to your client. that you might not say this to your customer. "You can trust me to help you with any recommendation I offer. I will never be primarily self-serving. I will be watching out for your interests, and when you benefit, I will benefit also."

The client is someone you guide. The client is someone you serve. A client is someone you protect.

Create Clients that Want to Meet *You*

How can you find clients who want to meet you? I'm going to give you a formula that you need to start considering for all your marketing communication and prospecting. This will also apply for the new world of communicating through video that we talked about earlier.

You will need to recognize in this hyper-dynamic, attention deficient modern world, this will be THE way things will be done in the very near future.

Remember how your non-client prospect thinks. Suppose it is I.

"I do not care to give you anything when you visit with me, do you know that? I don't care if you want to know my number of employees. I don't care if you want to know my revenue. I don't care if you need this to put a bid together. I don't care if such and such is your policy. I don't care how big you are. I don't care how important you are. I don't care how busy you are. I don't care. I don't have anything to give you. I must protect my own resources. Do you know that?"

"I have my needs and I will do anything I can to meet them. I care about ME."

So, if you want a meeting with me, your real obligation will be to guarantee to deliver something important to me, value, on the first encounter, second encounter, third encounter and beyond.

Consider a formula:

Value + value + value = Sales opportunity. You may then Upsell, or Down Sell

Then, your offer must cost less than the value you have and will deliver.

Then the process returns to the start. Here's what this means. You must commit to deliver value in no less than 3 encounters before you sell anything. Then, if the value materializes, if it's received and recognized as valuable, your prospect, now your client (as you have committed and are demonstrating your commitment to protect his or her interests) should be interested to become part of what you're offering because you've delivered significant value, and you know him enough where you can deliver something that he knows makes his life better. The model goes like this "Value, value, value, sell." Then you may, "Up-sell, down-sell." Even if the prospect didn't buy, you're not done. Maybe there's something else you can do for them, or maybe there's something you can do more of for them, because you've learned about them, and you win when the client receives and recognizes your value.

I can guarantee that he or she will look forward to meeting again.

How does you create and deliver value? How is it delivered if it is not your full product offering? It's really not that difficult. It comes in any one of these three forms.

It can be knowledge, relationships or perspective. That's all you've got. That's what they need, too.

- You want to give them how-to information that they don't have – something that is new to them that they need to know to do what they do in their world.

- You want to give them assessments. You want to help them learn about their own company in a way they couldn't have done it otherwise.

- You want to show them the common myths, the mistakes and traps they'll fall into if they follow common practices.

- You want to be able to show them competitive analysis or economic information.

- Round tables, webinars, and connectedness – something that allows them to notice that they need to be in a relationship with you, so important is the stuff you're providing.

Here's an idea that I always hear – and I hate it. It is an idea from an old economic system long gone. The idea is that you or any company should withhold your best information until you get paid.

I say give your best stuff first so that your prospect is fully aware of how valuable the impact your product will actually be, from experience. This will also clarify what they are paying for. **Besides, if what you gave them for free is that good, they'll know that what they pay for will be worth it.**

It's the old model that believes that if I have something and I give it to you then I've lost it. This is more accurate. In this world, if I have something and I give it to you, then we both have it. I'm expanding the value of everything and everyone I touch.

Today, you need to deliver these things continuously.

Key High Value Messaging: Express how Life will be Better

It is very important to be able to state your offer in a clear and irresistible (to your perfect client) manner effortlessly and quickly. If you really focus well, these prospects will experience a real connection. "He's/she's talking to me. I feel understood! I feel validated!"

Here are a few quick models of formats you may follow to construct and test your own offers. Each of these has been tested in situations from the classic elevator, to headlines for web landing pages.

Model # 1: Who, What, So What

"I provide {who's your audience} with
{what product or service} so that
{what difference will it make in their world}."

Notice that this example is focused on the difference you're offering will make in the world of a specific audience. Remember, no one cares about what you do. They care about what difference it makes in their world.

Examples:

> I provide tight margin contactors guaranteed delivery of high quality masonry materials so that they can reduce their masonry costs by 10% by eliminating wasted labor hours.

> **I provide authors, speakers and coaches with** the "10 Essential Steps" to becoming a millionaire sharing their advice and knowledge with the world.

Model #2: What, When, "Whew"
"My Clients receive {Results} in {Timeframe} without {Objection}."

Here's what you communicate: "What you get is this result, in this timeframe, without having to do the bad part. Be clear about the impact your product or service has on your customer, how long you expect it will take to get that result, and what they'll avoid if they choose to work with you instead of another.

Examples:

- My client's get hot, fresh pizza delivered to their door in 30 minutes or it's free.
- My clients learn to entertain others on a piano in 90 days without having to learn to read music.
- My clients run better, grow faster, and make more money within a single quarter without increasing their costs.

Model # 3: Great Benefit without Great Hassle
{Incredibly good impact} without {incredibly bad hassle}

This style of irresistible offer is only effective if you are very clear about your client's realized value and their strongest most common objections. (Isn't that what we all need?)

Here are a few examples:

- Have a Super Bowl Party for 50 friends at your home without the mess. (Caterer)

- Get twice as much done while doing half the work. (Productivity coach)

- Lose 30 pounds in 30 days without ever being hungry.

Most of us don't know how to give a compelling offer for what we do, so it takes us 10 minutes to describe what we do in a world where we need do it in 30 seconds, and if we're speaking to our perfect client they'll say, "Hey, I need to talk to you." Not because they need to buy something, but because they want to get better. They want the impact that will make life better.

The Pitch Anything model:

- For {audience}

- Who are dissatisfied with: {challenge}

- My product/service is: {offer}

- That provides: {activity}.

- Unlike: {current state}

- My product: {Differentiator}

This model comes from an incredible book, Pitch Anything, by Oren Klaff. (www.pitchanything.com)

Klaff uses the model effectively with even the most difficult audiences. It is designed to help you make a compelling offer in a very small amount of time, so that people can experience the benefit available to them.

It is extremely effective as an introduction to a presentation.

4 Keys to Create Clients that Want to Listen

How do you get people to keep listening and *wanting* to listen to you? You've met, even had a few meetings. Does your client want more of you, or are you having trouble getting the next meeting?

This problem is best solved if you continue to deliver real value in every meeting. Remember: Your client doesn't care about your agenda. He doesn't care if YOU need to meet him. He doesn't care if YOU need anything. (You're not there for you, anyway, right?)

Your client cares about how meeting with you is making his life better. That's all you really need to be concerned about, too.

Here are a few things you must provide to guarantee your clients will keep listening to you.

1. **Care**
    - This is big. Caring is not a game, nor is it a ploy (though demonstration of caring can be a skill that can be abused).

    - It is a genuine heart to heart, relationship-enhancing characteristic of your involvement in his or her life.

- Do you care about your client's life, your client's health, well-being, and success? This is foundational.

2. **Curiosity**
   - Are you curious about your client's business/ situation? Genuinely curious?
   - Do you wonder how he sees things? How things work
     in her world?
   - What inspires him? What she fears?
   - Why they do the things they do?
   - Genuine curiosity will keep you from having to script or control your meetings. Instead, you are able to powerfully address and respond to their concerns.

3. **Helpfulness**
   - Do you want to help solve client challenges? Or do you want to get a deal? Which is primary?
   - Whichever it is will become evident. Your client can tell.

4. **Perspective**
   - Perspective is the most under-delivered and unrecognized value that you can give your clients.
   - It is also one of the things they want most from you. It is important that you recognize this too.
   - Perspective is the key differentiator in your entire world. It is the power of you. It is made evident when you share your perspective.

- Clients don't know everything. Things are changing so rapidly they can't keep up.

- Every one of us has this thing called perspective, unique perspective, or expertise. But we tend to under-value it to our peril.

- Perspective isn't spouting your opinion. Properly shared perspective has a clear formula. It is you sharing from your experience:

    i. What others should pay attention to

    ii. What things mean

    iii. How things work

    iv. What will happen if . . .

Power of Perspective

I review the concept of perspective because it is so critically important.

What is perspective? It's the way we see something. My perspective is unique. Your perspective is unique. It is based on unique (and often vast) experience. The concept of perspective is comprised of how you and I see things differently, which is really cool because it means we're both right – from our perspective.

Here's what sharing your perspective is: telling people what to pay attention to, what things mean, how they work, and what will happen if… all based on what you've observed, noticed, learned, thought about, or whatever.

If you listen to experts in media interviews, this is the formula they use all the time.

Here's why your clients want your perspective: it provides them with a condensed version of what's going on in the world. It's really valuable because they don't have the bandwidth to do the study you've done and to synthesize the information like you have. Think about it.

Guarantee Clients that Want to Buy

When your client has wanted to meet with you, and then continued wanting to listen to you, and you have provided valuable perspective, you should be ready to make an intelligent and credible recommendation as to whether your client should buy something from you. This should be the natural result.

If you've set this up right, they're excited to be with you. You're delivering value all the time.

Your clients will be guaranteed to buy from you if:
- You have a high value solution to a real challenge.
  » It's a real deal. They acknowledge it. You acknowledge it.
  » You're delivering something they see as valuable. They see that. Yes?
  » You don't force anybody to buy anything because if there's a high valuable solution to a real challenge, it's automatic, which is what the second point says.
- The solution is worth a lot more than the real cost.
  » You don't force anybody to buy anything because if there's a high valuable solution to a real challenge, it's automatic.

» Why do people resist your offer or shop you after you buy? They don't believe there's enough value. Or, they don't understand where it is.

» They're not sure, so they have to go test it and see if somebody will give them a cheaper deal, because they don't know what they're getting from you.

» No one can resist the value purchase.

- You can guarantee the solution will work.

  » You should be able to guarantee everything you offer. If you offer an impact, you should be able to guarantee the impact. Why do I say that? If you can't do it, don't offer it. **Only offer what you know you can do. Only offer what you know your product does, and since you know it does it, you can guarantee it.**

  » It is bold to guarantee your results. It is important to guarantee your results. In the entire expert world, they're starting to guarantee their results. "If it doesn't work, you don't owe me anything. That would be a dishonor for me to take your money and not produce a result."

  » That doesn't mean you give them the money back for a building you constructed. It means you guarantee they get the result that you promised or else don't do business with them.

Make Your Own Real Contribution?
Comment on *The Coming Jobs War*
by Jim Clifton, from Gallup.

This book contends that the responsibility of a business owner, especially in a developed capitalist economy like the USA, has shifted. No longer can a business operator be considered responsible if he operates a profitable enterprise. It is not enough to just take care of business. Such practices may actually be detrimental to the economy at large, and, as a result, be ultimately detrimental to the enterprise you run.

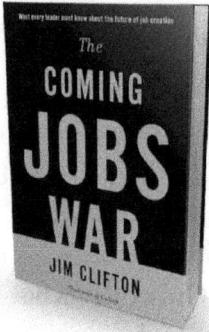

Clifton makes an irrefutable case that corporate health is promoted by a healthy economy. A healthy economy is dependent on GDP. This is the same for the world economy, as well. GDP is, at its core, the measure of the entire economic value available for all the people who live there. If the economic value of the entire country does not cover the needs of all the people who live there, it's done. It's finished. It's bankrupt. The same is true for a business enterprise too.

The world has three billion people looking for jobs. They need a good job. Meanwhile, only 1.2 billion jobs exist. That's the main reason for current worldwide unrest and revolution. If people can't eat, they can't be expected to sit still. With the Internet, anyone can see what someone else is doing, even across the ocean. So when revolution happens in one place, it's likely to incent another hungry people group to do the same.

Here is Clifton's Responsibility Changing Thesis for business owners: GDP is not created by you building your own empire with as few employees as you can. It is developed through the **creation of jobs.** Now, you thought it was okay for you to build your company and to maximize your personal earnings and then do no more. According to Gallop's massive research, you're setting yourself up for the collapse of a country that needs to develop more GDP, otherwise it will be taken over by countries like China that will have no trouble growing their own GDP because they have unlimited consumers and zero saturation.

Conclusion

"The best source and predictor
of new jobs is new customers."
—*Jim Clifton The Coming Jobs War*

Listen carefully. If you want to see your business thrive, and your lifestyle survive, you must take seriously your responsibility to grow America's GDP. To do this, you must do more than maximize your earnings. You must also maximize your value on your community.

Here's the bottom line: If you're not creating jobs, you're not creating GDP, and if you're not creating GDP, it's only a matter of time before we're sucking wind off of some other country that DOES build GDP.

The best source and predictor of new jobs is new customers.

That's why this book is so important. It makes sense, then, that it comes around full circle, too. Selling more, working less, having more fun is the best way to impact our world and our economy.

So I leave you with this challenge:

- Become better at selling. You must. It is life and life-giving for you and those you serve.

- Become better at connecting. Your happiness depends on strong human connections.

- Become better at delivering value. The world desperately needs your contributions.

Then, hire and inspire people to expand your reach. Create as many jobs as you can. The Secret? Clifton says it clearly. **"The best source and predictor of new jobs is new customers."**

This effort will be beneficial for the planet and for you. It will create a better lifestyle for you today, and for your children and grandchildren in the future.

You can do this. You're smart enough to do this. You work hard enough to do this.

Being a better salesperson isn't just about finding a way to sell more of whatever you are offering to your clients, or turning as many prospects as possible into these clients. Instead, it is about learning to make the connections, build the relationships, and offer the quality and value that not only was once the cornerstone of all enterprise in this country, but also is the basis by which you can create a successful and fulfilling life, both personally and professionally.

Of course you want to make money. That is one of the benefits of having a career. But it is only one. More importantly, you want to be the type of person that feels good about the money that you have made, and knows that you have earned it through natural, honest, and beneficial means rather than strong-arming or manipulating people. In the end, you need to remember that the first thing you sell to any prospect is yourself, and you must keep this personal transaction alive as long as you intend to have clients as part of your business and life.

Why not build relationships for a lifetime? Why not make it your goal to sell more, work less, and have more fun? You'll be making an essential and valuable contribution to yourself, your family, your community, and the world. It's a worthy pursuit.

CJ Coolidge

About the Author

CJ Coolidge is a sought-after international speaker and productivity expert who, for thirty years, has helped small businesses and Fortune companies achieve their goals. In his lectures and writings, he highlights the often-ignored connection between a company's people practices and its profitability goals, connecting them in a new paradigm: The People-Driven Business Model.

Since 1988, CJ has served as business performance advisor to Insperity (NYSE:NSP). As a young salesman, he generated $1 billion in revenues. His accounts were so profitable for so long that Insperity named its annual sales profitability award after him for nearly a decade.

CJ is founder and CEO of C4 Dynamics, a consulting and training company that has helped thousands of businesses improve their bottom line. In this breakthrough book, he explains his surprising and innovative insights.

CJ Coolidge is an international speaker and facilitator, offering talks, retreats, and workshops on topics related to this book.

For information, write or phone:

info@CJCoolidge.com
281.482.5586
www.cjcoolidge.com

Notes

Notes

Notes

Notes

Notes

Notes

Notes

Notes

Notes

Notes

Notes

Notes